# A FATHER'S TIME

## TODD C. ROBISON

ISBN-13: 978-0-9851538-0-9

# DEDICATION

This book is dedicated to my four children. All of you make me smile and have made me into a better man. Austin "The Bullet," Spirit "The Dominator," Elijah "The Firecracker," and last but not least, Lincoln "The Sensei." I love you all very much.

# CONTENTS

# ACKNOWLEDGMENTS

First, I thank my Triune God. God, as my father and creator, I thank you for being my sovereign authority over each and every one of life's situations. Jesus Christ, I cherish you as the sacrificial lamb of God. You came down to earth in the form of a man. You were born of a virgin and lived a sinless life (Matthew 1:18-25). Then, you went to the cross and gave your life as the ultimate sacrifice (John 3:16). You rose from the dead on the third day (Luke 24:6-7). You did what no one else could do. You are my Savior and I am eternally grateful. Then, you blessed every believer with the Holy Spirit. The Holy Spirit that lives in me and through me. Another gift from heaven is the Holy scriptures. The truth contained in your word is priceless (Psalms 1). Heavenly Father, this book would not have been possible without your presence in my life.

In addition, I'd like to thank Christine Hodge, who was a tremendous editor and advisor throughout the entire process. Without your guidance, I never would have finished this project. A big thanks to Matthew Kinne who helped me early on and kept me moving forward..

I'd like to mention my beloved wife, Tracy. You are one of those people who has allowed me to grow and improve as a man, husband, father and friend over the years. I treasure our relationship like a fine wine that keeps gaining value and beauty over time.

# INTRODUCTION

*Behold, children are a gift of the Lord, The fruit of the womb is a reward. Like arrows in the hand of a warrior, So are the children of one's youth.*

(Psalm 127:3-4 New American Standard Bible)

Working as a professional educator, I was first exposed to children's needs that were not being met. I spent my first years as an educator with private schools. I made the transition into public education to make more money. The majority of my time teaching was spent with elementary and junior high students.

One of the most challenging and rewarding assignments I had was to teach an opportunity class. This class was designed for the behavior-problem students. It was their last opportunity to straighten up before getting sent out of the district. It was an in-house continuation school. My job was to keep them in line, along with getting them up-to-speed for high school. While working with these young people, their desperate need for attention was hard to ignore. I found that a high number of the children experiencing the most difficulties in school had one thing in common, or lacked one key figure in their lives. They did not have a dad who was actively participating in their daily lives. I felt the need to do something, and that is when I began working on this book.

# HEY DAD

Hey Dad, where you at?
I woke up for school today and all I saw was your hat.
While you were gone I had baseball practice and I
was first up to bat.
Homerun! Center left.  What do you think about
that?
I asked mom where you went and she just said,
"He's  not coming back."
Left?  What? Where did you go dad? Where you at?
No more kids stuff dad, I am learning to drive now.
I am trying to learn how to drive a clutch and don't
know where second gear is at.
I got a job to pay for my first car,
It's a nice little Fiat,
I am not sure how to change the oil just yet.
If you were around you'd know how.
I am sure of that.
Well, Dad I am off to college today.
Going to study Humanities at UCLA.
I've never been to L.A.
Hey, dad I was wondering......Where's uncle Ray?
Does he still live down there with my cousin Jay?
No, really Dad, where did you go?
I need some help bad, right now I'm hooked on blow.
My friends all took off,
I can't find a job, or clean clothes.
People laugh at me and say I'm a slob.
And now I am starting to bleed out my nose.
I needed you back then, and I need you now.

How could you leave us Dad?
Please just tell me how.
It is super cold out tonight
and I can't find a spot to lay down.
A place to get warm
anywhere inside, just not the wet ground.
Hey Dad, I am off the drugs now.
Sober for ten days. It's true.
It is weird getting clean, I never had a clue.
My mind starts to wander
and fixates on what I can't do.
Then all of the sudden I start thinking of you.
I start to break down and tears fill my eyes.
Where did you go dad?  Just tell me why?
I was approached by a street preacher yesterday.
Who looked into my eyes.
He told me about Jesus
and the laying down of his life.
Jesus died on the cross,
shed his blood and paid the ultimate price.
The gift of salvation only comes through his sacrifice.
I learned that I am important to him.
I can be forgiven of my sins. And so can you.
No matter where I go, no matter what I do.
The Lord will never leave me dad. Not like you.
I know grown men aren't supposed to cry.
But if I hold onto this anger,
it it will eat me up inside.
So I forgive you Dad,
for leaving without even a goodbye.

# EVERYDAY HEROES

My son began training with a local track coach a few years ago. My initial expectation was to drop him off at practice and then pick him up when it ended each day. We did this for the first week. That following weekend, my wife and I received an e-mail from the track coach. He was requesting our presence at practice and asked us to take a more active role with our son and his training. At first, I wasn't sure what the coach meant by this. My wife and I discussed the email and what our son's coach was asking us to do. I went down to practice after work the following Monday to ask the coach what he needed me to do. I said that I knew very little about track and felt ill-equipped to offer any coaching advice. He responded, " I need you to be here even if you are only watching. Just the fact that you are here, speaks volumes in the life of your son." It all began to make sense. The more I thought about what the coach had said, the more I agreed with him. I was blown away by the wisdom and truth in the words he had shared with me. I did what the coach requested and I was amazed at the results that followed. I showed up at many of the practices throughout my son's track career. I attended most of his track meets. If I was running late, my son would call to see when I was going to show up. My son's track coach is much more than just a coach. He is a mentor with a heart of gold. His name is Ed Italo. He is most definitely an everyday hero that has made a difference in the life of my son.

# 1 PARENTING IS LIKE A RACE

*Do you not know that those who run in a race all run, but only one receives the prize? Run in such a way that you may win.*

1 Corinthians 9:24

Many of us have been taught to believe that we are dads for approximately 18 years. Then, our job as a father ends. At that point, we become "empty nesters." Are you one of those guys? Are you looking forward to the time when your kids turn 18? Are you looking forward to the day when you can give them the boot and see what they can do? This particular school of thought is what I describe as sprint-parenting. The sprint starts on the day our children are born. From that day on, we are looking toward the finish line. Is this the best perspective to have in raising our kids?

In the world of running, sprinters are able to see the finish line from where they start the race. They use starting blocks to give them an extra push. Once the race begins, every ounce of energy is directed toward the finish line. Each and every muscle is working at its maximum potential for that short amount of time. One hundred meters is a sprinting distance that we can see in a snapshot. We can see the entire race in a matter of seconds. These races are straight forward. There are no turns, no changing lanes and no time to adjust to circumstances. The intensity needed to win these races is unbelievable. Making one or two mistakes in any part of the race can be catastrophic.

Distance runners, by contrast, have a more long-term perspective. When I talk about distance runners, I am referring to ½ milers, milers, and greater distances. Starting blocks are not typically used in distance races. Again, the start is very important, but the same explosive beginning is not necessary to win. These racers have a more strategic and methodical perspective. Having a strategy is necessary to be successful, but there is definitely time to make multiple adjustments before the race is over. The level of focus needed in a distance race is comparable to a sprint, but the biggest difference is the duration of that focus. A sprinter has to focus for a matter of seconds, while distance runners must remain focused for several minutes at a time.

The importance of planning is the same in both sprinting and distant races. Planning involves setting goals and laying out the steps needed to reach those goals. Planning is necessary so when we are running, our energies are applied in the most efficient ways possible.

Our responsibility as dads will last until we die. It is a lifelong commitment to our children. No matter how old they are, they are still watching us and need us to be available for them. Our roles will change, but our love and availability needs to be consistent.

My dad used to wrestle with me when I was really young. As I got older, he would help me with math problems, spelling and other homework. I relied on his superior intellect to help me at that point. While in high school, my parents separated. I chose to move 6 hours away and live with my mother. Living so far away from my dad was very difficult. I missed seeing him on a regular basis. During the fall, he would drive 4-6 hours to football games and watch me in action. The priceless gift he gave me, by attending my games, was his time. Seeing him there on the sidelines was awesome. I remember watching and waiting for him to arrive. A few years later, when I met my wife and needed to earn money, he gave me a job working for his company. This opportunity allowed me to begin making money when I needed it most. After earning and saving enough money to buy a new car, he told me to buy a house instead of a car. He said that a house was a much better way to invest my money. I took his advice and purchased my first home at the age of 23. That first home purchase helped to pay for my some of my college education. Now, as a married father of four, I call my dad on a weekly basis for advice on things ranging from work, contentment, being married and money. My needs have changed,  but I still need to know that my dad is there for me.  I love my dad.

Looking at the relationship I have with my father, you can see the advantage of having a long-term perspective versus a short-term one.  Blending the fire and intensity of a sprinter with the strategy and vision of a distance runner is the ideal combination. Throughout this book, we will continue to find the balance between these two parenting strategies.

# 2 DAILY ROUTINES

*Sow your seed in the morning, and do not be idle in the evening, for you do not know whether morning or evening sowing will succeed, or whether both of them alike will be good.*

Ecclesiastes 11:6

Our daily routines reveal what we value the most. By looking at what we do every day and how much time we spend on each activity, we are able to see what is important to us. Where do you spend your time in any given day? Where do I spend my time?

Let's break a 24-hour period into three parts. We need approximately eight hours of sleep, eight hours for work, and eight hours for everything else.  Starting with an average weekday, list out everything you do. Begin with the moment you wake up, and end with the time you lay your head down on the pillow to go to sleep. I will use one of my normal workdays as an example,

## Current Weekday Activities

| Time | Activity/Description |
|------|---------------------|
| 4:35 a.m. | Wake up |
| 4:35-4:55 | Shower, shave, etc. |
| 4:55-5:00 | Gather up computer/lunch |
| 5:00-6:30 | Commute to Long Beach |
| 6:30-7:30 | Settle in-Coffee/Devotion |
| 7:30-11:30 | Check e-mails/phone calls, etc. |
| 11:30-12:00 | Lunch |
| 12:00-3:00 | Back to work-paperwork, etc. |
| 3:00-6:00 | Commute back home |
| 6:00-6:30 | Stop by my son's track practice |
| 6:30-6:35 | Greet wife and kids (hugs/kisses) |
| 6:35-6:50 | Play with 5 and 8 year old |

| 6:50-7:30 | Eat Dinner |
|---|---|
| 7:30-8:30 | Discuss day and just talk |
| 8:30-9:00 | Devotion |
| 9:00-10:00 | Settle Down and sleep |

Now cluster these activities into three categories and calculate the amount of time spent on each.

|  | **Minutes** | **Hours** |
|---|---|---|
| Work | 780 | 13 |
| Family | 210 | 3.5 |
| Personal | 60 | 1 |
| **Totals** | **1050** | **17.5** |

What is going on here? Am I actually spending approximately two-thirds of my waking hours at work? Is that good or bad? Well, if I want to be remembered for putting work before everything else, I would say that these results are fantastic. Consistently spending this amount of time at work shows that my top priority is work. If, on the other hand, I am striving to spend more quality time with my wife and kids, I have some serious changes to make. Seeing this makes me feel guilty. I am earning money. I am also able to accomplish most of my tasks at work, but who is missing in this equation?  Could it be my family? I guess I could hide behind the good ole phrase "I'm just providing for my family," but the financial side is only one piece of the puzzle. Identifying key areas that need improvement is one of the first steps. If I had never listed out my daily activities like this, I may have never seen the need for change. We all have different levels of tolerance in regards to work and family. I can tolerate working 12 hours a day for now, but I am not content with maintaining this level of work for more than a few more years, or even months. What is your tolerance of hours spent at work? The better question is, how much time can your children tolerate being away from their dad? After looking at our weekday routine and reflecting on the results we get, the next thing we will do is take a look at how we spend our weekends. Are you ready?

Follow the same specific pattern of listing each activity, time of day, and amount spent doing each one. It is up to you whether you list out a Saturday or Sunday. If you have a unique schedule, just pick one of your days off. I have listed out one of my routine Saturdays to see how it looks.

## Current Weekend Activities

| Time | Activity/Description |
|------|---------------------|
| 6:30-8:00a.m. | Wake up/Coffee/Devotion |
| 8:00-10:00 | Drive Son to track meet |
| 10:00-11:30 | Watch my son race |
| 11:30-12:30 | Drive home |
| 12:30-1:00 | Stop at beach to play |
| 1:00-2:00 | Finish the drive home |
| 2:00-2:30 | Lunch |
| 2:30-5:30 | Watch movies with kids |
| 5:30-6:00 | Drive oldest son to movies |
| 6:00-7:30 | Go to work |
| 7:30-8:00 | Pick oldest son up from movies |
| 8:00-8:30 | Drive home |
| 8:30-9:00 | Lay down with kids |
| 9:00-9:30 | Drive son's girlfriend home |
| 9:30-10:30 | Watch movies with my wife |

|          | Minutes | Hours |
|----------|---------|-------|
| Work     | 90      | 1.5   |
| Family   | 720     | 12    |
| Personal | 150     | 2.5   |
| **Totals** | **960** | **16** |

When we compare total hours spent at work, I spend 13 hours a day during the week, and only 90 minutes on a Saturday. During the week, I had 11 hours left in my 24-hour period when I got home from work. I slept approximately eight hours, which left me three hours for everyone and everything else. Looking at my Saturday routine, I worked only 90 minutes, with my standard eight hours of sleep. I am left with 14.5 hours for free time. I spent approximately 12 hours with my family on Saturday. I drove my children around town, watched my oldest son race, watched movies and just enjoyed the time away from work.

You have had an opportunity to see how I spend my time. Now look at the totals of your workday alongside the totals of your day off. Look at what you are doing with the extra time that is not spent at work. Is it wasted? Has your idle time increased? Did you wake up earlier or later than normal? Did your TV time increase? Clustering into the three categories of *work, personal,* and *family* is very helpful.

# 3 THE PERFECT DAY

*This is the day which the Lord has made; Let us rejoice and be glad in it.*

Psalm 118:24

This next exercise can be very fun. We will use our imagination to picture our idea of a perfect day. Without a road map and final destination, we don't know where we are going.  Our perfect days will be the goals to strive for. Be as specific as possible on these ideal situations so they become real and achievable.

Since we are already familiar with tracking and writing down our current daily routines, we can use that format for  our perfect days too. The first one to picture is a work day. Close your eyes and imagine how your day begins. Then progress through your day, stopping to have meals and continuing on until you find yourself back in bed laying down before going to sleep. This may take a few tries, and some perseverance, but don't give up. Once you have closed your eyes and seen the perfect work day, write it down and assign each activity a specific amount of time.

If you are unable to picture your perfect day, then write down what you think it might look like. If you want, take a more linear approach  by using a timeline. Perhaps you could use your daily routines sheet and just change the order and/or times given to each activity. If you prefer to draw small pictures, do that. It might turn out looking like a comic strip.

Don't limit yourself based on people's views of normal or what is expected. Get crazy and picture your perfect work day. The only limitations are that it must be a total of 24 hours, generate enough money to support your family, and a set amount of time for sleeping. Everything else is wide open.

I have listed out my perfect workday activities for your  reference.

**Perfect Weekday Activities**

| Time | Activity/Description |
|------|---------------------|
| 4:30 a.m. | Wake up/Devotion |
| 7:30-11:30 | E-mails/phone calls, etc. |
| 12:00-1:00 | Lunch |
| 1:00-2:00 | E-mails/phone calls, etc. |
| 2:00-2:30 | Pick up kids from school |
| 2:30-6:00 | Play with kids |
| 6:00-7:00 | Eat dinner |
| 7:00-8:30 | Play some more |
| 8:30-10:30 | Devotion/bedtime |

Now cluster these activities into 3 categories

|        | Minutes | Hours |
|--------|---------|-------|
| Work   | 360     | 6     |
| Family | 480     | 8     |

| Personal | 180 | 3 |
|---|---|---|
| **Totals** | **1020** | **17** |

I currently spend 12 hours at work, but with my perfect workday, it's only six hours. Working only six hours a day may not be realistic right now, but why not have it as a goal?

I had four hours of family time on my actual work day, while in my picture perfect day, I spent twice as much time with my family.

I have been spending an average of one hour a day on personal activities, but when I imagine a perfect day, I end up with three hours of personal time.

The conclusion:  With six hours less spent at work, I have tripled my personal time from one hour a day to three. This has taken only two of the six extra hours outside of work which leaves  me spending twice as much time with my family. How about you? What are your comparisons looking like? I know my example has come out looking very clean with even hours. Yours may or may not come out evenly. You might have 15 minutes hanging over in one area, or find yourself coming up short 30 minutes in a different area. It's okay. The goal is to have an accurate starting point that adds up to a 24-hour period.

If you happen to work at a job that does not allow you to shift your hours or work less, take a closer look at what you are doing once you get home from work. Is your time being spent on things that bring you and your family closer together, or are you pursuing your own interests that take away even more time from your kids? Are you too exhausted to participate in the activities your kids are doing? Are you still thinking about work when you get home? These are just a few questions that may help us think about our children more every day.

Once you have completed a perfect work day, it's time to picture the perfect day off. This one is another step out into the unknown, because work is not even a consideration. A 24-hour period and your need for sleep are the only parameters set in stone.

**Perfect Weekend Activities**

| Time | Activity/Description |
|------|---------------------|
| 6:30-7:00 a.m. | Wake up/Devotion/Coffee |
| 7:00-11:00 | Play with the kids |
| 11:00-12:30 | Lunch |

| 12:30-2:30 | Yard work |
| 2:30-7:30 | Play with kids (games/ sports) |
| 7:30-8:00 | Dinner |
| 8:00-11:00 | Watch television/play with kids |
| 9:30-10:30 | Fall asleep on the couch |

Now cluster these activities into 3 categories

|  | **Minutes** | **Hours** |
|---|---|---|
| Work | 0 | 0 |
| Family | 720 | 12 |
| Personal | 150 | 2.5 |
| **Totals** | **870** | **14.5** |

Now get both of your current routines (weekday and weekend) and your perfect days in a hard copy form so you can put them side-by-side. Begin glancing back and forth between the two work days. Then do the same with your days off. What jumps out at you? Do you feel anxious when you do this? Are you disappointed? Write down the differences that you see on each of your days. Then, cluster the activities into our three categories: work, personal and family. Do some digging into each of your lists to highlight which activities you want to start working on first.

My perfect weekend is very similar to my current weekend. The one key ingredient that is missing in my perfect day is work. Hah! That's beautiful, isn't it? I did have yard work written down in the afternoon, right after lunch, for two hours, but I enjoy it so much I don't consider it work. My family time has remained the same. My personal time is the same as well. The greatest obstacle I have had to tackle in recent years, is keeping a handle on my personal time. I have been known to throw myself into different sports and activities that end up taking huge amounts of time away from my wife and kids. I get all fired up, and then I look around to see that I am all by myself, chasing the next thing. If you find yourself in a similar predicament, please take the time to assess who and what you are giving your time to. As children, life seemed to revolve around us. As fathers, it revolves around our loved ones. We are here to serve and love the ones we care about.  Our own wants and desires become secondary to meeting both the physical and emotional needs of our families.

# EVERYDAY HEROES

A friend of mine works on cars for a living. He is married with children and has a lot of time on his hands. He planned out his daily routines before starting his own business. My friend works an average of 30 hours a week. He has mapped out a business plan that allows him to make enough money to pay the bills, turn a profit, be the best at what he does, and have plenty of time left for his wife and kids. He loves his family and has made decisions based on that love. With his extra time, he volunteers for local youth organizations and gives generously to those in need. My friend is planning on working a 30-hour work week until he is unable to work anymore. Retirement is not even a consideration for him. This particular friend of mine is an everyday hero who is giving his family the time and attention they deserve. His name is Eric Hodge. He is an everyday hero.

# 4 BUILDING BRIDGES

*And for this purpose also I labor, striving according to His power, which mightily works within me.*

Colossians 1:29

The gap between what we are doing now and what we dream of doing will be linked together by daily and weekly steps. I have to recognize that I am not decreasing my work hours from 12 to six overnight. This will be a gradual change over months and years. I can start with 5-10 minute increments at a time. Perhaps I can get to work 10 minutes earlier and leave 10 minutes earlier. I could eliminate one of my breaks, or shorten my lunch by ten minutes in order to allow myself to leave that much earlier.

If I am serious about cutting the time I spend at work in half, I will have to be persistent and think long term. What if I extend this change in behavior over three years? When I do that, I now have a goal of two hours less spent at work each day by the end of a year. I would be working five 10-hour days a week. My 60-hour week is now down to 50. Once I get that far, the next step is more realistic. After two years I am down to 40 hours a week. Finally, after all the blood, sweat and tears, I am holding it down with a 30-hour work week. Yeah!

I encourage you to start small in your changes. It will snowball into something great. The extra five or 10 minutes at home with your children, could be the time you see one of them take their first steps, ride their bike without training wheels or any number of small victories in the life of a child. Small changes every day will turn into big changes over time.

The main point is to use your perfect days as a specific goal, break it down into small pieces, and then take daily steps toward your goal. Write your daily goals down and keep them somewhere you can see throughout the day. Time is ticking. How and where you spend your time is up to you.

# 5 BREAKING OLD PATTERNS

*Therefore if any man is in Christ, he is a new creature; the old things passed away; behold, new things have come.*

2 Corinthians 5:17

Looking at our past behaviors is one way to break old patterns. Our past experiences have shaped who we are today. We are not limited by our past, but we look back and learn from it. Changing the habits that undermine our families is what we need to do.

Let's begin with identifying the strengths and weaknesses in our daily routines. We will build on our strengths by staying consistent, and eliminate our weaknesses by replacing those activities with better ones. We need to change our habits and adjust our focus by zooming in on our children who are pleading for our attention.

"Backwards mapping" was a teaching strategy I learned in college. The way we planned our lessons was to start with the goal in mind. Having already written down your perfect days, you have a goal/map in front of you. Then, we map out a route, or plan, which includes steps we need to take in reaching our goal. Without a solid goal or permanent idea, the direction is going to change countless times. If you change the direction too many times you end up in a place that may be completely wrong. Having a clear and definite goal is one of the key ingredients in cooking up the type of love our children are hungering for. Persistence and perseverance are necessary to stay on the path that brings us closer to our kids.

Another way to apply this backwards mapping model is to have "breaking the pattern" as our goal. You get to choose each pattern that you personally feel needs to be broken. Then, attack each of them, one at a time. First, identify it. Then, take logical steps to break it. Once you have ended a negative pattern, replace that pattern with a better one. Talking with family and friends you admire and trust will be a priceless resource in helping you see the habits that need changing. Knowing where you don't want to end up is just as important as having a clear final destination.

Looking back on my earliest childhood memories, I vividly remember peddling my bicycle with my dad holding on to the seat. I was learning to ride my bike without training wheels. I remember the feeling like it was yesterday. I was going as straight as possible. A moment later, my dad was not holding on any more. He said, "just keep going" and I did. I will never forget the rush of excitement I felt in those moments. I was riding my bike without training wheels! It clicked. I got it, and my dad was there to see it.

I have to say that as a kid, I truly felt loved. I was quiet in comparison to my older brother, but very content. I just sat back and watched my brother put on a show for everyone to see. Being the center of attention was something he thrived on. I preferred being in the audience and watching things happen around me.

As I got older I really enjoyed school. I liked the structure and achieving recognition for a job well done. Family, church, school, vacations and friends all seemed to be perfectly intact until I went off to Ventura High School as a freshman. I saw it coming, but when it hit, I was crushed. At the end of my freshman year, my parents made the announcement of their separation. I did not know how to respond. I was given an option at this point. I could move away with mom, or stay with dad and my older brother. I was informed that my brother had already chosen to stay with dad. I decided to go and live with mom. Multiple things influenced this decision. In the end, I felt that my mother should not be moving away to a strange town all by herself.

It was my junior or senior year of high school when my dad came up for a visit. We went for a drive and the bomb was dropped. In a solemn voice dad told me, "Your mother and I are getting a divorce." There was a rush of emotions that flooded me and then it was over. I knew it was coming in the back of my mind, but hearing the word "divorce" carried an enormous amount of weight with it. The finality of this statement was a hard pill to swallow.

I was already entrenched in a vicious cycle of drug abuse when I heard the news. The only way I saw to cope with this tragedy was to numb out. I continued this destructive behavior with a group of friends who were very eager to do the same. Toward the end of my senior year, a beautiful young lady transferred to our school. In a small school like ours, nothing like this went unnoticed. Well, eventually she called me and asked me to take her out on a date. We went out a few times and were inseparable shortly thereafter.

I am now 37 years old. My wife is 36. We have 4 children. Yes, I married my high school sweetheart. My wife and I both had parents who loved us very much. We also share the experience of watching a divorce tear our families apart. It is a real tragedy that far too many children have to endure. We are trying to break this pattern in our family. My wife and I continue to love each other in ways that our children can both see and feel. I continue to strive to be the very best husband to my wife. I am far from perfect, but I will never stop trying. My goal is to be the husband she reads about in fairy tales- someone who makes her feel like a queen. She needs a man who treats her with respect and admiration. A man who leads his family with strength, love and consistency is the type of father and husband I am working to become.

Work is the great distraction in life for men. When the kids are crazy, I can go to work. When my wife needs me, I can go to work. When everything is falling apart, I can go to work. So what does work become for me? It becomes an escape. What the heck am I trying to escape from anyway? Am I trying to escape from the ones I love? Am I trying to avoid responsibilities? I feel the pull of my job every day. Is there something else to take care of at the shop? Can I process just this one more order? Yes. The more important questions are, "What am I working for? Who am I working for? Where are the most important people in my life?" They are at home, waiting anxiously for me. At work I have supervisors, managers and co-workers looking to me to get things done in the most efficient ways possible. What do I value the most? Who do I value the most? How do I rank these different people that I interact with on a daily basis? This takes some soul searching. The amount of time we give to each of these different people is a good indicator of who we care for most.

Let's rank the top five people in our lives.

Mine                    Yours

#1) Jesus Christ        #1)

#2) Wife                    #2)

#3) Kids                    #3)

#4) Friends                 #4)

#5) Work Associates         #5)

I have my Lord and Savior as number one because he is my number one. Without Jesus in my life, I would be a total disaster. He continues to shape me into a better man through the power of the Holy Spirit and the truth contained in the Bible. I am banking on the fact that I will be with him for eternity. I just have to be patient.

Next on my list is my wife. Yes, she is my love. We have our ups and downs, but we have each other's back. She is my loving friend and perfect match.  My wife is an amazing woman who is quick to let me know when I have allowed her to slip down on my list of people. It is sad, but true. If it wasn't for the love and support of my wife, I would be a wreck.

Number three on my list is my children. With children, I have more of a direction in my life. Provider, father, husband, mentor, teacher, friend, advisor and companion are just some of the roles I find myself in as a father. I love it. Being a good father and husband are the two most difficult jobs I have ever had.

Number four is where I have ranked my friends. I used to put them at number one as a youngster in high school. For me it was a mistake; many of my choices that were influenced by my friends have been detrimental to the current situations I find myself in. God was always there for me, I just chose not to look to him.

My work associates are number five. Work associates and friends may sometimes overlap, but the people at work are still very important to me. I rank them fifth because my family is directly impacted by how I interact with my co-workers. If I am disrespectful, irresponsible and lazy, it will directly impact my ability to provide for my family.

I find that many times throughout the years, my number four and number five have ranked up at the very top. It takes constant effort to keep all of my relationships going. They might even change numerous times throughout life. Just look at them as motivators. Let your list motivate you to do and make the very best choices possible in every situation. If your kids don't rank high on your list, move them up in the rankings. Elevate them in both your heart and mind. Do whatever it takes.

# 6 BEING HONEST

*Do not lie to one another, since you laid aside the old self with its evil practices, and have put on the new self who is being renewed to a true knowledge according to the image of the One who created him*

Colossians 3:9-10

Sometimes I find myself saying something that sounds very good, when it may actually be a lie. Take this statement as an example: "Hey Johnny, I will come by your practice today if I get off early." In the back of your mind you know you are swamped at work and most likely won't make it to the practice. Just don't say it if you can't follow through. It hurts you and your children. Being a man of your word is something that never loses value. We all want people to listen and trust what we say. Better yet, we all want our kids to trust what we say as being true.  Your actions will reflect your core beliefs and values. If I say that I cherish the weekends in order to spend time with my kids, but end up golfing or motorcycle riding for most of every Saturday, am I being honest? If the things you enjoy most take you away from your kids, find something you can do together. If you value your own personal time above all else, just say it. Whether you say it or not, you kids probably already know. If you can't be honest with yourself, who can you be honest with? If I continually make excuses for my mistakes and shortcomings, I will never grow or improve in those areas. I have to be completely honest with myself and those around me.

Saying something and not following through is a subtle serpent. It will slither into daily situations at the drop of a hat. Even if it sounds great, but is impossible, bite your tongue and don't say it.

It was my oldest son's first day of kindergarten. I love to participate in school activities, so my wife and I both took him to his classroom. He was nervous, along with my wife and I. As I began to see numerous parents drift out of the room, my anxiety level shot through the roof. "What am I going to do?" "How is my son going to react as I try to leave?" These questions were racing through my mind. I ultimately made a bad decision and told my son, "I have to go to the bathroom, I'll be right back." I lied to him in order to eliminate a big crying scene as I left him at his first day of kindergarten. I felt a mix of emotions as I left his campus that morning. I felt guilty for lying to him. In a twisted way, I was also pleased with myself for making a smooth exit. I was hoping he would forget my *lie* from earlier that morning. I told my wife what I had done and we drove off with each other, thinking and wishing we could make this first day of school for our son go perfectly. As it turns out, my boy did not forget my *lie.* One of the first things out of his mouth when we picked him up was, "Why did you lie to me dad? You said you were going to the bathroom and you never came back!" It ripped my heart out to hear him say that. To this day, I still feel terrible every time this subject comes up in a conversation.

We may think we can pull the wool over our kids' eyes. We might even succeed on occasion, but it is the wrong thing to do. I have not forgotten the broken promises of my father. A child's number one hero is "good ole dad" for most of their lives. We can't let our kids down by lying to them. I'm not talking about Santa Claus or the Tooth Fairy or the Easter Bunny. Those are all childhood fantasies that can be shared with your kids if you see fit. I am talking about real life issues; the day-to-day interactions that shape all of our kids and give them a consistent foundation of trust, or distrust that will carry them onward and upward throughout their later years in life.

Don't lie, but don't go to the other extreme and be so brutally honest that hurtful things are said in the spirit of truth. I have always tried to be real with my kids, especially my oldest son. I think I overcompensated in this area, due to the fact that my own parents did not communicate in the most effective ways. They just avoided conversations about taboo subjects. Sex, drugs, and death were subjects we did not speak about very often. In regards to sex, it was "don't do it until you are married." Our discussion on drugs was "don't do them, they are dangerous, and might even kill you." Death, well, we spoke of death when someone died, and that was it. The final decision on how to deal with sticky subjects in your household is up to you.  Think it through beforehand. Think of the things you wished you knew but didn't. Then when the time and age of your kids is appropriate, address each issue in a straight-forward, loving way.

On the other hand, as a young and naïve father, I thought it best to shoot straight and give my children as much information on these three subjects as I could. The theory behind this was to give them the information and allow them to use it and access the information when necessary. As children develop, they are able to process and interpret information differently at various ages. Consider this when bringing up different issues. I believe I made some mistakes with my oldest by sharing too much information before he was ready for it.

Talk to your wife about your long and short term goals with your children. Practice honesty with her. It takes practice to be open and transparent. If you want your kids to really see you for who you are, start with you wife.  Your wife deserves the same level of respect and openness, if not more. You need to be an open book. Let your family  see you cry once in a while. Real men do cry.

Another option is to seek out a successful father for advice. I am not talking about financially successful. What I mean is, find a dad who gives his children the time, love and attention that they deserve. Ask as many questions as possible to draw on his experiences. Ask him how he deals with sticking to what he says. Seek out other fathers from your work or church. I had a another father share with me how doing the little things consistently, for him, has lead to great things over time. I can apply that to loving my children consistently. Starting the day by waking them up with a kiss, and tucking them into bed with another kiss. I can strive to be consistent in being there for my kids each and every day.

One more place that seems to be forgotten in our quest for more knowledge is the retired community. Older people have done and seen things that we will never have the opportunity to do. Honesty is a valued principle that has definitely stood the test of time. Ask your grandparents, or someone else's grandparents how important the principle of honesty was for them in their own lives. I have found the talks with my grandmother, over the years, extremely rewarding. She loves sharing stories from her childhood. I get to hear about her career outside the home, along with her struggles of being a mother. She has told me about losing her dad at a young age, and the hurt she has felt over the years. She is a golden nugget in the area of life experiences. I treasure the times we have spent together talking about anything and everything.

# EVERYDAY HEROES

A friend of mine works for a large corporation. He has worked for this particular company for many years. Early on in his career he decided to be there for his children. Over the years, many different opportunities have come his way. Some of them offered more money, but required more time away from his family. My friend has stayed true to his convictions and remained in positions that have enabled him to be there for his kids. We talk about all the sporting events he goes to each weekend. Watching his kids compete and have fun on the weekends is a high priority in his life. My friend has told me multiple times to consider my career decisions in the same way. I appreciate his advice. I have a lot of respect for my friend. He has resisted the temptation to chase after things that would take him away from his family. I know his wife and children love and appreciate everything he does for them. His name is Richard Canet. He is a true everyday hero.

# 7 BE INTERESTED IN WHAT YOUR KIDS ARE DOING

*Do nothing from selfishness or empty conceipt, but with humility of mind let each of you regard one another as more important than himself; do not merely look out for your own personal interests, but also the interest of others.*

Philippians 2:3-4

*"See that you do not despise one of these little ones, for I say to you that their angels in heaven continually see the face of My Father who is in heaven."*

Matthew 18:10

Take an interest in your kids' activities. Start by asking your kids what they love to do. Watch them play with their friends. Set aside some time to sit and watch your kids in action. Go to their sporting events and practices. Watch to see how and what they do out there on the playground or athletic field. Dive into their world, and don't forget about school. Talk to their teachers. Help them with homework. Make the journey with them. If you are married with multiple children, the balancing act is a tricky one, but very possible. If you have junior high/high school-aged children, it is not too late. You have to try ten times harder to break into their world, or at least struggle to stay inside their world. They will argue and fight it at first, but they will truly appreciate your effort and love for the rest of their lives.

Asking your kids what they love to do may seem strange. I know you already have your own ideas, but it is not about you. Getting your child's input is huge. Tapping into their world is the goal. The younger they are, the more likely they will be to let you in with open arms.

If you have a 5-year-old, you may already see how their favorite activities change daily. At this age, your kids will shout what they want at the top of their lungs. The beautiful thing about this is how it removes a lot of the guess work on your end. My 5-year-old son will begin chanting what he wants to do over and over again until he gets a response from me. I never taught him how to chant, it is a skill that he, along with every other preschooler, has developed naturally. Lincoln loves to dance. He is always looking for opportunities to show others how well he can dance. Lincoln plans on becoming a famous dancer.

My second youngest child is eight. He is just a few steps ahead of his younger brother. For the most part, he continues to get my attention with his shouts or by grabbing me with his bare hands. If I give him the opportunity, he is happy to plan out our weekends from start to finish. He is a little firecracker. He has bursts of energy that run me into the ground. Elijah enjoys playing sports. His favorite is baseball. Elijah plans to be a professional baseball player.

Being able to communicate more effectively, as a 15-year-old, is something my daughter really enjoys, and takes full advantage of. She is very smart and beautiful. I cherish these qualities about her. My daughter doesn't ask to spend time with me anymore, but I don't stop asking her. There are times when it takes a little extra patience on my part to understand what she truly wants and needs. When it gets to be too much , I consult my wife. My lovely wife is the female expert in my house. I team up with her as much as possible in relating to our daughter. My wife and daughter disagree at times, but they relate to each other in ways that only a mother and daughter are able to. Spirit is wonderful. She is a phenomenal poet with a very kind heart.

When I look at my oldest, I see the face of a young man staring back at me. He is 17. It is like pulling teeth to get him to talk most of the time. I am challenged by his silence, but I also recognize that he needs just as much love as my other children. He just doesn't say it anymore. Austin is level-headed and very intelligent. He has an ear for great music that he is always happy to share with me. He is the first of four wonderful gifts from God.

No matter what the age of your children, you need to know about their interests. It is not too late. Ask them what they like to do more than anything else. Ask them where they like to spend their time. Listen intently to them. Find a place with no distractions. Sit down with your son or daughter and ask these questions in a loving and gentle way. Look at them as they are giving you their answer. Be sure to validate what they are saying with head nods and encouraging words. Ask them to be as specific as possible. Explain to them that the reason for asking them these questions is for you to become a better father. Once you hear their answer, repeat it back to them to get confirmation that what you heard from them was accurate. Next, you should write it down. You don't want to mistake or misinterpret what they are communicating to you.

Watching your children play with their friends is very helpful in finding out their interests. It is a difficult task to tackle, but worth your while. Seeing how they fall in the rankings with their friends is a unique experience. Are they the alpha dog, the runt or someone in the middle just trying to fit in. Take some time to really watch and study them. Study them and learn about them like you are studying for a final exam. Be intensely intentional.

Over the years, I have chaperoned for a few different church trips and school activities. The great thing about these trips was seeing my children interact with others in different settings. How my son carries himself around his friends is fun to watch. He is quiet and reserved when I am with him, but I can hear him get loud and boisterous when I am walk away. When my son and his friends start in with "talking trash" he says just enough to keep them at bay. This is a unique skill to acquire at any age. Digging into what makes his buddies tick helps me understand their frame of mind and what kind of influence they might have on my son. I am quick to ask each of his friends about each of their family and living situations. Most of them have the common complaints of their dads working too much, along with mom calling far too often to see where they are.

I have seen my kids change their demeanor at the drop of a hat. One second, they are laughing with their friends, and the next, they clam up and don't want to be bothered. My two oldest are really good at this one. I poke and prod them until they open up, or I sometimes just give them space. When we have some alone time to talk about this exact thing, my son usually responds with, "I'm just tired." So I just start asking him what some of his closest friends have been up to. (Knowing family backgrounds gives you a connection which helps in getting them to open up.) I just ask, "Hey, what is Jake up to?" or "Where has Micah been lately?" or "Who is dating who?" Nine times out of ten, he begins telling me about at least one or two of his friends and what the most recent drama has been. Young people love to talk, you just have to tap into the subjects that spark their interest the most. The number one topic is friends.

Next time you take your children to the park, pay close attention. Are they wanting you to join in the fun? If they are looking at you, you know what you need to do. Get up and join in.

I just recently got home from a long day of work and commuting. I was absolutely exhausted. I sat on a lawn chair for a few minutes. My eight-year-old asked if I wanted to play in the castle. I said, "not right now," because I needed to rest. He asked me a few more times, and eventually I got up and slowly meandered over to the castle. The latch on the castle door was locked, so I reached over and unlocked it. He ducked his head slightly to get through, while I crawled on my belly through the door. Once inside, it felt like I was back in medieval times, defending our castle against the invading giants. I told him what I had imagined and he jumped on board. We picked up acorns and began throwing them over the castle walls to keep the giants at bay. His little brother saw all the fun we were having, and came running over to join in. This is just a small example of a "golden nugget" I was able to share with my two youngest children. Now, I could have just as easily sat in my chair and came up with a few more excuses and he would have probably given up on me. Speaking from the heart, I hope he never stops asking me to come and play. I hope he never gives up on me. If you are joining in the fun with your kids, you will eventually see when their eyes light up with pure joy. I love to be there and see this when it happens. Watching a young child grow in enthusiasm and strength is a beautiful thing. When you see them out on the basketball court, or out on the track or soccer field, pay close attention. You can watch them go in and out of the "zone." I use the word zone, to describe not only the twinkle in their eyes, but also the full body experience of adrenaline. Go to enough practices, dance recitals, performances, games, competitions or school activities, and you will see what I am talking about. Mention it to your kid after one of these events. Tell them that you were able see the excitement on their face at a specific point in time, and see how they react. They love to know that you are not only attending these events, but that you are really watching them.

My oldest loves for me to stay and watch his practices. He constantly looks over to see if I am paying attention. I recall him asking me not to bring my books to his practices. He said I would end up reading my book instead of watching him practice. Multiple times after hearing him tell me, I would go to grab a newspaper or book on the way out the door, and I would remember those words he said.

My daughter gets frustrated with me and my socializing with other parents. She will glance over at me during her practices, and if she sees me talking with other parents during practice, she asks me to focus more on her. My daughter's request is very important to me so I make adjustments right away. I treasure her honesty and I can always count on her to tell me when I forget and become distracted during her practices.

Moving on down the line, my 8-year-old is very bold in his requests. He just shouts, " Watch me daddy, watch me daddy, watch me daddy!" until I acknowledge him. If I don't respond, he runs up to me with a very angry look on his face, "You're not watching me daddy." As I reflect back on this, it just tears my heart out. It is not okay to think that some phone call, or trivial conversation, can keep me from loving him and giving him the attention he deserves. If my son cares enough to say something, I should love him enough to listen.

Lastly, I have my 5-year-old. He communicates with his eyes, hands, tears, tantrums and any other objects that fill his needs at the time. His strategy in gaining my attention is to grab me, try to move me, grunt loudly in my face, cry or scream "dada" with an increasing noise level until acknowledged. Once he has my attention, he will take off in the direction of what he wants, looking back over his shoulder every few steps, to confirm I am following him. I just love that little guy.

School is another huge part of your child's life. All of us went through school with varying degrees of success. Some of us loved it, while others just hated it. Let your kid know how you felt about school as a youngster. Dig down deep in order to explain why you felt a certain way about your school experience. Did your opinion and participation in school change as you got older? What type of influences caused you to change? Mention any of the teachers that really stick out in your mind. Tell your child the reasons that these particular teachers come to mind. Were they superb teachers, or terrible ones? Did they help or hinder your education? Your kids will love hearing about your school experiences. Be sure to stress the importance of school to them. Find out who their teachers are and attend the open houses throughout the year. Stop by the classroom on occasion. It makes me smile just thinking about my kids sitting in class, toughing their way through it, just like I did as a kid. As a former teacher, I definitely appreciated having an open line of communication with parents. The students who had little or no parent involvement struggled the most. Their challenges were not limited to schoolwork, but even simple interactions with the other children.

Once upon a time, my oldest son was sent home for fighting at school. I felt disappointed when I received the phone call from my wife. Before getting too worked up, I waited to hear the story from my son. I gave him a chance to present his side, then I shared what I knew. I asked him how it started. Who said what? Who threw the first punch? I also asked him if it was necessary to use his fists in this situation? Did it solve the problem? If you find yourself in a situation, remember that the answer to some of these questions may come about after a few days, weeks or months, but it is good to follow up. Be sure to tell your son or daughter that in order to learn from our mistakes, we need to analyze them closely. If there are any inconsistencies in my son's story, I find them. If anything does not add up right, I ask my son why things don't add up. I allow him a little room to squirm and then I nail him down. Encouraging our little ones to accept responsibility for their actions is important in helping them to grow into responsible adults.

Children can see right through most of our inconsistencies with little or no effort. They can see if you don't like what you are doing. They can tell if you would rather be somewhere else doing something different. If you are not enjoying the time spent with your kids, they know it. Don't fake it! You will be hurting them more than you know. I have been guilty of this numerous times. I remember sitting out in the back yard recently while my daughter was trying to get me to watch her hula hoop. I was looking at my daughter, but actually looking through her in a daze. She told me, "Dad, you're not really watching me, you're just day dreaming." She was right. The act I had put on didn't work. Why was I putting on an act in the first place? Nothing was more important at that moment than watching my daughter. A few days ago when I was driving and thinking about the reports due at work, my daughter was talking to me. My "uh huh" responses only lasted a few minutes, and then she caught me by saying, "Dad, you're not even listening to me. You are just saying 'uh huh,' even when it doesn't make sense." She caught me and I apologized. It takes practice, but being in the moment with your kids is so important in strengthening your relationship.

If you are unable to be there for any of their events, be sure to ask your child for a play-by-play description of what happened. If you are not there for them, let your child know that you wish you could have been. Asking them these types of questions lets them feel your desire to be with them.

# 8 UNCONDITIONAL LOVE

*Love is patient, love is kind and is not jealous; love does not brag and is not arrogant, does not act unbecomingly; it does not seek its own, is not provoked, does not take into account a wrong suffered, does not rejoice in unrighteousness, but rejoices with the truth; bears all things, believes all things, hopes all things, endures all things.*

1 Corinthians 13:4-7

Loving your children for who and what they are is loving them unconditionally. We all want our children to accomplish great things in their lives. We want them to do better and achieve more than we have. We have our personal wants and desires for each of our kids. I have to tell to my kids that the love I have for them is not ever going to change. Whether they fit into my idea of success, I will still love them the same. I have to tell them this on a regular basis. The second step is living out my love for them in ways that they see and feel as being true. A great

example of unconditional love is found in the book of
Luke.

The Parable of the Lost Son

[11]Jesus continued: "There was a man who had two sons.
[12]The younger one said to his father, 'Father, give me my
share of the estate.' So he divided his property between
them.

[13]"Not long after that, the younger son got together all he
had, set off for a distant country and there squandered
his wealth in wild living. [14]After he had spent everything,
there was a severe famine in that whole country, and he
began to be in need. [15]So he went and hired himself out
to a citizen of that country, who sent him to his fields to
feed pigs. [16]He longed to fill his stomach with the pods
that the pigs were eating, but no one gave him anything.

[17]"When he came to his senses, he said, 'How many of my
father's hired men have food to spare, and here I am
starving to death! [18]I will set out and go back to my father
and say to him: Father, I have sinned against heaven and
against you. [19]I am no longer worthy to be called your
son; make me like one of your hired men.' [20]So he got up
and went to his father.

"But while he was still a long way off, his father saw
him and was filled with compassion for him; he ran to his
son, threw his arms around him and kissed him.

[21]"The son said to him, 'Father, I have sinned against
heaven and against you. I am no longer worthy to be
called your son.[a]'

[22]"But the father said to his servants, 'Quick! Bring the best robe and put it on him. Put a ring on his finger and sandals on his feet. [23]Bring the fattened calf and kill it. Let's have a feast and celebrate. [24]For this son of mine was dead and is alive again; he was lost and is found.' So they began to celebrate.

[25]"Meanwhile, the older son was in the field. When he came near the house, he heard music and dancing. [26]So he called one of the servants and asked him what was going on. [27]'Your brother has come,' he replied, 'and your father has killed the fattened calf because he has him back safe and sound.'

[28]"The older brother became angry and refused to go in. So his father went out and pleaded with him. [29]But he answered his father, 'Look! All these years I've been slaving for you and never disobeyed your orders. Yet you never gave me even a young goat so I could celebrate with my friends. [30]But when this son of yours who has squandered your property with prostitutes comes home, you kill the fattened calf for him!'

[31]" 'My son,' the father said, 'you are always with me, and everything I have is yours. [32]But we had to celebrate and be glad, because this brother of yours was dead and is alive again; he was lost and is found.' "

(Luke 15:11-32 New International Version).


This parable paints a beautiful picture of the saving grace offered to us by Jesus Christ. We, as sinners, long to go out and experience all the fleeting pleasures that the world has to offer. Getting caught up in always having more is an easy trap to fall into. The younger son eventually saw the emptiness that this life has to offer apart from a saving relationship with his father. Jesus Christ offers us a forgiveness and openness just like the father in this parable. The younger son knew his father growing up, but made decisions to walk away and try things on his own. He failed, and when he needed his dad to be there for him, he was. His father celebrated his son's return with a party. We can learn countless lessons from this parable. The greatest lesson is that Jesus Christ offers us this kind of unconditional love. The only way to really show this kind of love to our own children is to follow this example.

If my son asked me for his inheritance, I would have to think about it long and hard. For starters, there would not be a whole lot for me to hand over to him. Secondly, if I decided to give him his money/inheritance, would I be willing to take him back home with open arms after he squandered the money away? It would take some time to work through, but I would definitely welcome him back home. How do I love my kids like this? I have to look at them and love them with my heart, and not just my intellect and my ideas of success. I need to love them as people who are living and learning and making their way in the same world I am continuously trying to figure out.

In this parable, the son veered off course and eventually chose to come home. What if one of our children goes off in the wrong direction and chooses not to come home? What if they drift so far out that they actually lose their way? What do we do? The best answer I have for you is found in another parable at the beginning of Luke.

The Lost Sheep

[4] "What man among you, if he has a hundred sheep and has lost one of them, does not leave the ninety-nine in the open pasture, and go after the one which is lost, until he finds it?

[5] "And when he has found it, he lays it on his shoulders, rejoicing.

[6] "And when he comes home, he calls together his friends and his neighbours, saying to them, 'Rejoice with me, for I have found my sheep which was lost!"

[7] "I tell you that in the same way, there will be more joy in heaven over one sinner who repents, than over ninety-nine righteous persons who need not repentence."

(Luke 15:4-7, New American Standard Bible).


When we lose one of our children to the dangers and temptations of this world, we are hurt and disappointed. We have to dig deep to consider what we need to do in the best interest of our children. Some situations may warrant us letting our kids struggle through them. While other life choices may bring our loved ones into a pit of despair that they are unable to climb out of on there own. We, as fathers, need to be ready and willing to search them out like a lost sheep and bring them back into the fold. If we love them, we will teach and reach out to them in love.

# 9 GOT TIME? NOW WHAT?

*This you know, my beloved brethren. But everyone must be quick to hear, slow to speak and slow to anger;*

James 1:19

You have the evening set aside to spend with your son or daughter. You have decided to drive them to the next town about 20 minutes away. You both get into the car, buckle up, and hit the road. Depending on the age of your child, the conversation will vary. If it is uncomfortable silence, turn on the music ever so lightly. Ask them  about their sleep last night, school, friends, sports, teachers, etc. If they are opening up to you, make sure the music is turned off completely to enable you to hear each and every detail they share. Think of this like taking notes in a lecture. Granted, you can't write down what you are hearing while driving, but think of what they are saying. This time in the car is another golden nugget. Treat your time together with respect and care.

You arrive at your destination and your child has a look of disappointment on their face. You ask, "What's wrong?" He/she responds, "I just came here last week with Mike, it's boring." You have to choose quickly in how to respond to this lack of enthusiasm coming from your kid.

1) You can tell them to deal with it and smile, or you are both going home.

2) You can ask them what they would rather do instead.

3) You can tell them that they are an ungrateful little brat.

4) You can ask them to go in with you and try to enjoy the time you both have together.

No matter what response you choose, keep your cool. Getting a little friction is par for the course. Don't get frustrated. The idea is not to create the perfect situation. The idea is to spend time together in order to better understand and love your child. Try your best not to lose sight of that.

Getting the time with your kids is the first step. Allowing the magic to happen takes patience. Keep in mind the short and long term goals you have set for you and your kids. Don't be afraid to let your kids in on your goals. Let them know what it is you are striving for. Ask them to remind you.

Once you have time away with your kids, keep it free from distractions. Leave your cell phone at home (if your job will allow). Yes that's right. Since you are away from the distractions, try not to bring those same distractions along with you. I know how difficult it is when I get a text message and I feel the urge to answer it right away. I have to turn it off, or just leave it on the kitchen table. Otherwise, I end up glancing at my phone every few minutes, preoccupied with what might be said in the next message. I know it sounds crazy, but it happens more than I like to admit.

# 10 ESTABLISHING NEW HABITS AND TRADITIONS

*So then, brethren, stand firm and hold to the traditions which you were taught, whether by word of mouth or by letter from us.*

2 Thessalonians 2:15

What habits or traditions have been passed down to you in your family? Are any of them based on your heritage and where your ancestors came from?

Something I remember doing with my grandfather on my mother's side was going over to his house on the weekends and having bratwurst. Grandpa Ted would barbeque them up and serve them with a healthy portion of sauerkraut. In keeping with tradition, my mother has continued cooking brats on holidays and family gatherings.

I once heard an idea about a way to establish a healthy family tradition. I call it the "Plate of Honor." Ours is red. This "Plate of Honor" is given to someone in the family at meal time. Their food is served on this plate and set in front of them. This plate signifies that they are the special one at the table. Each of the other members in the family takes a turn saying how and why they love the person who has gotten the red plate. I was extremely excited when I heard this idea. I tried it and it was a huge success. Now my family and I use the red plate regularly. Lately, my 5-year-old throws a fit whenever he sees anyone else getting the red plate. He doesn't quite understand it all, but he does know that he wants to be the center of attention.

A family is like a house. We need a solid foundation. This foundation needs to be level, weight bearing, reinforced with steel, and formed out to the right dimensions. Do you get the idea that the foundation is important? Try to build a house without a solid, well-prepped foundation and see what happens. Disaster is inevitable. You have principles and beliefs that guide you in your everyday decisions. I have principles and beliefs that may greatly differ from yours, along with some that may be in common. Each of these principles are important for us to teach and build upon.

Principles are guiding forces that have stood the test of time. Principles such as integrity, honesty, loyalty, industriousness, enthusiasm and perseverance have stood the test of time. These same principles are being tested right now by many different people and organizations. You, as the leader of your family, have the responsibility of showing and living by the principles you teach your children. Go and ask your father and/or grandfather about principles. Ask them how certain principles have guided them in their lives. Ask them which particular principles were most important in raising their own children. How important were the existence of principles in raising you?

Repetition brings about habits. Habits passed down through the generations become traditions, and principles are the guiding force behind them all. What kind of habits, traditions and guiding principles do you want to continue in your family? What new habits, traditions and principles are you willing to start?

Let's list out five habits or traditions you currently have established. Then list out five that you would like to implement in the near future. (Be sure to list out the guiding principles for each.)

## Habits/Traditions

## Already in existence with guiding principles

1_____

_____

_____

2_____

_____

_____

3_____

_____

_____

4_____

_____

_____

5_____

_____

_____

## Habits/Traditions

## I want to start with guiding principles

1_____

_____

_____

2_____

_____

_____

3_____

_____

_____

4_____

_____

_____

5_____

_____

_____

The habits and traditions you pass on to your children are your legacy. Ask your wife and kids for some help on this if you want. They are the ones who will be most impacted.

Establishing new traditions will take discipline and dedication. Your traditions can be once a year, once a month, once a week, or even once a day. You set the parameters. Once you have succeeded in one or more areas, share your ideas with others.

# 11 RECOGNIZING OPPORTUNITIES

*Be on the alert, stand firm in the faith, act like men, be strong.*
*Let all that you do be done in love.*

1 Corinthians 16:13-14

Let's say you are at an outdoor event and you see an old friend or someone from work, what do you do? You might greet them with a hand shake and shift into "work mode."  A second later, you feel your little one tugging at your shirt and saying, "Daddy, daddy, will you take me to the park?" Your response could be, "Not now son, I am talking to someone. Go ahead and I will watch you from here." You continue on with the conversation and you see out of the corner of your eye, your son walking away sulkily. You see him slowly snap out of it as he gets to the playground and starts climbing around.

You just missed it. You failed to recognize a golden opportunity. Your son, the only one like him in this world, had invited you into his world, and you said "No." You may or may not get many more of these opportunities. You might be thinking, "I can't always go and play with him every time he asks me." Is that true? Maybe you were in an important discussion about someone at work, or about the new account that he landed and you are anxious to give him a few words of advice. If he is your co-worker, you can most likely talk about this subject on Monday, right? The final decision is up to you. I just want to stress that we all might be missing opportunities without even knowing it.

Opportunities will come and go. We need to try and catch them before they pass us by. Here are some ways we can be more adept in noticing opportunities to share time with our kids?

1. Listen to your kids when they are talking to you.
2. Pay attention to see what makes them smile.
3. Remember your kids are only young once, make the most of it.
4. Think about what you cherish most about your childhood. Then share it with your kids.
5. Talk to your wife about what she thinks they need.

6. When your kids have some free time- choose to spend it with them.

7. When you have some free time-choose to spend it with your kids

8. When you are in the middle of a task or conversation and your kids break in to ask you something, stop and give your children the attention they are begging you for.

9. Talk to other fathers who seem to have more time for their kids- ask them how they do it.

10. Think of how your kids will remember you when they are older. Were you there the first days of school? Were your there for their first home run? Were you there when they graduated? Were you there when they needed you most?

# 12 DISTANCE PARENTING

## The Second Letter of Paul to Timothy

*To Timothy, my beloved son: Grace, mercy and peace from God the father and Christ Jesus our Lord, I thank God , whom I serve with a clear conscience the way my forefathers did, as I constantly remember you in my prayers night and day, longing to see you, even as I recall your tears, so that I may be filled with joy.*

2 Timothy 2-4

*Train up a child in the way he should go, Even when he is old he will not depart from it.*

Proverbs 22:6

If you are in the military, jail, prison or in a career that keeps you away from your family, I want to start by encouraging you. There is always hope for you and your children.  There are many ways to stay connected with them from a distance.  Technology has a lot to offer in this area. Computers are one of the quickest ways to communicate, second only to telephones. Making use of these different resources can allow you to express interest in what your children are doing. If you are able to write letters, e-mail, make phone calls or have short visits with your kids, ask them what they love most. Pay close attention and respond to what they tell you out of love and respect. The distance and limited time you have together may actually give you more time to process what your kids tell you. Taking full advantage of every minute you share with your kids is important.

Having a solid and healthy relationship with those people who are closest to your kids can enable you to stay connected. If you don't have a connection with someone close to your children, try to reach out and ask them to help repair or re-establish a connection with your kids. Ask the people closest to your kids to attend sporting events and practices. Follow up by getting daily, weekly and monthly updates on what your kids are doing. If you are able to get updates on your loved ones, save them. This information is helpful in knowing what to talk about if those awkward moments of silence creep up on you while you are talking with your kids.

Get a hold of every picture, letter and artwork related to your kids that you can find. Each of these items is a connection. Talk to your child about each picture you have of them. If you were with them when the picture was taken, remind them of those times together and express the joy and love you feel when you think about them. Get a copy of every report card. Go down the list, one class at a time. Find out why their grades are so high or low. Take more time to point out the good grades than you do the lower ones. Build on their strengths. Let them know you are proud of them. Ask about each teacher. Find out about how old and how friendly the teachers are. Do they have any favorites? How many teacher's pets are in the class, and is your child one of them? Simple questions that bring you into the classroom with them are phenomenal. Take the energy and passion you have for your own interests, and focus it on your kids. They are looking to you. They need you.

# 13 INTERNALIZING WHAT YOU'VE LEARNED

*But prove yourselves doers of the word, and not merely hearers
who delude themselves.*

James 1:22

Take what you have learned in bite-size pieces. If I
attack a large task all at once, I don't deal with it very
well. Before I am anywhere near completion, I am usually
overwhelmed and slow to move forward. But, in contrast,
if I take the same exact situation and focus on bite-size
chunks, one at a time, I am able to deal with it in a much
more effective way. We need to look at improving the

relationships with our kids in the same way. One step at a time.

Repetition is the key to improving the amount of time spent with your kids. Like with anything new, practicing and repeating the basics consistently brings about change and improvements. Let's say that your children are not responding as quickly, or in the ways you had hoped they would. You can't give up. Be patient. If you  neglected your child in the past, repairs will take a while. Staying consistent by following through with what you say will show them you care. Having perseverance and patience will be necessary to accomplish your goals with your kids.

Effectively communicating your feelings and ideas with the ones you love is what it ultimately comes down to. Another word I can interchange with effective is successful. If you are able to successfully communicate your love with your children, your relationships will flourish.

The first steps are the hardest, but I promise you that once you begin reaching out to your kids with loving arms and heartfelt words, and offering them the gift of your time, the rewards will keep coming.  Be a dad, be a hero, be everything your kids want you to be.

# ADDITIONAL RESOURCES

**Music-** "Father of Mine," by Everclear

"Cats in the Cradle," by Harry Chapin

"The Living Years," by Mike and the Mechanics

**Books-** "Big Russ and Me," by Tim Russert

"Bringing up Boys," by James Dobson

"Don't Waste your Life," by John Piper

"Shepherding a Child's heart," by Ted Tripp

"Uncommon," by Tony Dungy

**Movies-** The Blind Side

Fireproof

Courageous

**Family Friendly Magazines-** Highlights

**Social Networking Websites that your kids are probably using-**Facebook

Thank you for setting aside the time to read this book on behalf of your children. I hope and pray that you and your family will be blessed by spending more time together. The smallest moments can be the greatest opportunities for loving and learning.

Todd C. Robison

Made in the USA
Charleston, SC
06 January 2013